LEARN FROM MY MISTAKES AND SUCCEED WITH EASE!
TOP 10 BUSINESS BLUNDERS TO AVOID.

WHATEVER YOU DO, DON'T DO WHAT I DID!

RALPH SKRZYPCZAK

WHATEVER YOU DO, DON'T DO WHAT I DID! OFFERS READERS
ESSENTIAL INSIGHTS INTO THE TOP 10 MISTAKES TO AVOID IN
THE REALM OF GENERAL BUSINESS PRACTICES, PROVIDING
INVALUABLE GUIDANCE FOR NAVIGATING THE PROFESSIONAL WORLD
WITH CONFIDENCE AND PROFICIENCY.

LEARN FROM MY MISTAKES AND SUCCEED WITH EASE!
TOP 10 BUSINESS BLUNDERS TO AVOID.

WHATEVER YOU DO, DON'T DO WHAT I DID!

RALPH SKRZYPCZAK

WHATEVER YOU DO, DON'T DO WHAT I DID! OFFERS READERS
ESSENTIAL INSIGHTS INTO THE TOP 10 MISTAKES TO AVOID IN THE
REALM OF GENERAL BUSINESS PRACTICES, PROVIDING INVALUABLE
GUIDANCE FOR NAVIGATING THE PROFESSIONAL WORLD WITH
CONFIDENCE AND PROFICIENCY.

Legal & Copyright

Whatever You Do, Don't Do What I Did!

Written by Ralph Skrzypczak

Published by Counsel Wolf Books, an imprint of ATLB Productions

First Edition 2025

ISBN: 979-8-9989933-1-2

Cover & Interior Design by Counsel Wolf Creative

Preface

Whatever You Do, Don't Do What I Did!

By Ralph Skrzypczak.

This book has been created as a short digestible and practical guide. There are 10 main topics broken into 10 chapters. With a final chapter on action steps. My suggestion, is to read or listen all the way through once, and then over the course of 2 weeks focus on one chapter per work day and read or listen to one chapter before work. If you are reading to this, as a print book, pdf, or epub they can be marked up in a reader for notes specific to you, however an audiobook is great for the car to help you focus.

Special Thanks and Dedications

To my parents John and Joanna Skrzypczak for being there when there wasn't even a there to be at.

To Gregory Lynch for being the first teacher to pivot me in the right direction!

To Peter Meisel for listening to me and showing me how to Mambo #5 worldwide.

To Terence A. Donnelly for being Batman to my Robin in college showbiz life lessoning.

To Barry M. Goldwater Jr. for your indispensable wisdom, grit, and pragmatism.

To Grant and Elena Cardone for giving me permission to be 10X Obsessed.

To Brandon and Natalie Dawson for breaking my points and being the wise ventures'.

To Jon Taffer for public scream therapy and a bar rescued.

Mostly to you the reader. You have helped me in the biggest way possible and I hope that this book helps to inspire you to continue on regardless of any adversity or whoever may yell in your face. Follow these amazing people for more inspiration and give me a follow on any or all of the socials! And thank you again for reading!

Table of Contents

Introduction: Steering Clear of Common Pitfalls

Concept 1: Embracing a Mindset of Continuous Growth

Start the journey with the belief that each experience is a building block to greater achievements. Embracing a mindset of continuous growth opens up a world of possibilities and opportunities. It's about viewing challenges as stepping stones, not stumbling blocks. When we approach life with this mindset, we invite progress and success into our lives. By recognizing that every setback is a lesson in disguise, we can transform adversity into strength. Each new endeavor becomes an adventure to learn, grow, and achieve. Whether it's personal or professional growth, the pursuit of improvement is a lifelong commitment. It means understanding that failure is not a destination but a temporary detour on the journey toward excellence. Embracing continuous growth empowers us to rise above limitations and surpass our own expectations. It's a testament to our willingness to evolve, adapt, and thrive in the face of adversity. This mindset encourages resilience and fosters an unwavering determination to overcome obstacles. It fuels a passion for exploration and innovation, propelling us toward uncharted territories of success and fulfillment. Embracing continuous growth also instills a sense of purpose and self-assurance, igniting the spark of creativity and ingenuity within us. It nudges us to seek new experiences, broaden our horizons, and shatter self-imposed boundaries. As we embrace this mindset, we unleash our full potential and unlock the doors to endless possibilities. Remember, the journey of continuous growth isn't about perfection; it's about progress. It acknowledges that we are always a work in progress, constantly evolving and refining ourselves. With each step forward, we gain invaluable insights, skills, and wisdom. It's a journey of self-discovery and self-mastery, illuminating the path to personal and professional fulfillment.

Concept 2: Cultivating Resilience and Adaptability

In the realm of business and personal growth, resilience and adaptability emerge as indispensable traits that pave the path to success. Cultivating resilience involves developing the capacity to bounce back from setbacks, challenges, and failures with unwavering determination and optimism. It is about reframing obstacles as opportunities for growth, realizing that every setback is a stepping stone toward greater achievements. Practicing resilience also entails embracing change and unpredictability without losing sight of one's core values and aspirations.

Adaptability, on the other hand, embodies the willingness to evolve and recalibrate amidst shifting circumstances. It encompasses openness to new ideas, flexibility in approach, and an eagerness to embrace innovation. Embracing adaptability means being open to constructive feedback, learning from experiences, and remaining agile in the face of evolving market demands. It requires the ability to swiftly pivot strategies and capitalize on emerging trends while maintaining authenticity and integrity.

As we delve deeper into the concept of cultivating resilience and adaptability, it becomes evident that these traits are not only fundamental to individual growth but also essential for fostering resilient, adaptive organizational cultures. Organizations characterized by resilience exhibit a collective strength in navigating adversities, responding to change, and thriving amidst turbulent market conditions. On the other hand, adaptable organizations demonstrate the agility to innovate, pivot, and seize new opportunities, thereby maintaining a competitive edge in dynamic landscapes.

Moreover, the cultivation of resilience and adaptability fosters a culture of empowerment and forward momentum. It encourages teams and individuals to perceive challenges as catalysts for innovation, creativity, and collaboration. By fostering a climate where resilience and adaptability are celebrated and nurtured, organizations cultivate a workforce that is primed to overcome obstacles, drive positive change, and fortify the organization's foundation against uncertainty.

Furthermore, the intertwining nature of resilience and adaptability reinforces the notion that these qualities are symbiotic. Building resilience nurtures adaptability, and being adaptable fuels resilience. This synergy propels individuals and organizations to not only weather storms but to emerge stronger, more innovative, and more attuned to the ever-evolving landscape of business and opportunity.

In essence, cultivating resilience and adaptability forms the bedrock upon which transformative journeys are paved. They infuse endeavors with a spirit of possibility, enabling individuals and organizations to transcend limitations, redefine success, and etch their mark on the tapestry of achievement.

Concept 3: Setting the Stage for an Empowering Journey

As we embark on this empowering journey, it's important to acknowledge the significance of setting the stage for success. This chapter serves as a pivotal moment for embracing the potential that lies ahead, and it is essential to approach it with boundless optimism and unwavering determination. The stage we set today will lay the foundation for a future brimming with possibilities and triumphs.

To set the stage for an empowering journey, we must first cultivate a mindset of abundance and opportunity. Embracing a positive outlook and believing in the endless potential for growth and success can act as the propeller for our aspirations. When we approach our endeavors with the conviction that the universe is conspiring in our favor, we unlock the ability to manifest inspiring outcomes beyond our wildest dreams.

Furthermore, setting the stage for an empowering journey entails creating a supportive network of individuals who uplift and inspire us. Surrounding ourselves with like-minded visionaries and mentors who exude positivity and resilience fortifies our spirit and fuels our ambition. These connections serve as pillars of strength and wisdom, enriching our journey with invaluable guidance and encouragement.

Another integral aspect of setting the stage for an empowering journey is fostering an environment that nurtures creativity and innovation. By cultivating a space that encourages out-of-the-box thinking and celebrates diverse perspectives, we unlock the potential for groundbreaking ideas and transformative solutions. This environment becomes the fertile ground where innovation thrives and revolutionizes the landscape of our aspirations.

Moreover, embracing the essence of gratitude and mindfulness lays a crucial foundation for an empowering journey. When we acknowledge and appreciate the blessings, opportunities, and experiences that enrich our lives, we infuse our journey with a profound sense of purpose and fulfillment. Practicing mindfulness allows us to savor the present moment and be fully immersed in the wondrous unfolding of our odyssey.

In essence, setting the stage for an empowering journey is a deliberate and exhilarating endeavor. It encompasses the convergence of proactive mindset, supportive networks, innovative environments, and mindful appreciation. As we delve into the chapters that await, let us embrace the profound impact of setting the stage today for the extraordinary expedition that awaits tomorrow.

Chapter 1: Avoiding the Trap of Perfectionism

Core Idea 1: Embracing Imperfection: The Beauty in Flaws

Embracing imperfection is the cornerstone of personal and professional growth. When we allow ourselves to let go of the illusion of flawlessness, we open the door to true creativity, progress, and fulfillment. It's important to recognize that setting unrealistic standards and striving for flawlessness can hinder our ability to make meaningful progress. True success doesn't lie in perfection but in the resilience and courage to move forward despite our imperfections.

Each one of us is on a unique journey filled with twists, turns, and surprises. It's these unique imperfections that make our journey truly ours. Embracing these imperfections allows us to celebrate our individuality and express ourselves authentically. When we let go of the need to be perfect, we free ourselves from the constraints of fear and self-doubt, paving the way for innovation and genuine connection.

Consider the beauty of imperfections in nature—the asymmetrical petals of a flower, the irregular patterns of a tree's bark. These imperfections are what make each element of nature exquisite and captivating. In the same way, embracing imperfection in our endeavors can lead to unexpected and remarkable outcomes. By acknowledging and accepting our flaws, we empower ourselves to approach challenges with creativity and resilience, ultimately reaching new heights of achievement.

The journey toward embracing imperfection requires a mindset shift—a conscious choice to view imperfections as opportunities rather than setbacks. Instead of being discouraged by mistakes, we can learn from them and use them as stepping stones toward growth. This shift in perspective allows us to see the beauty in the process, rather than fixating solely on the end result. In doing so, we cultivate a sense of curiosity and adaptability that fuels our progress.

So, let's celebrate the beauty in our flaws and imperfections. Let's cherish the uniqueness of our journeys and recognize that it's these very imperfections that add depth, character, and authenticity to everything we do. By embracing imperfection, we pave the way for a more fulfilling and enriching path forward—one that is rich with learning, growth, and boundless possibility.

Core Idea 2: Progress Over Perfection: Celebrating Small Wins

Striving for perfection can be a daunting task, often leading to feelings of frustration and disappointment. However, by shifting our focus from achieving perfection to celebrating the progress we make, we can find renewed motivation and joy in our endeavors. Each small step forward is a testament to our dedication and resilience. It's important to acknowledge and appreciate these victories, no matter how insignificant they may seem at first glance. Whether it's completing a challenging task or learning a new skill, every accomplishment deserves recognition. By celebrating these small wins, we cultivate a positive mindset that propels us further towards our goals. Embracing the journey rather than fixating on the destination allows us to savor the process and experience fulfillment along the way. As we celebrate each milestone achieved, we infuse our efforts with purpose and passion, creating momentum that propels us toward even greater success. Furthermore, recognizing our progress fosters a sense of gratitude and self-confidence, reinforcing our belief in our abilities and strengths. This, in turn, empowers us to face future challenges with optimism and determination. Small wins are the building blocks of significant achievements. They provide us with the encouragement and validation we need to continue our pursuit of excellence. It's through acknowledging and commemorating these victories that we fuel our own growth and development. In doing so, we inspire others to adopt a similar mindset, fostering a supportive environment where everyone's accomplishments are acknowledged and celebrated. In essence, by focusing on progress over perfection and embracing the value of small wins, we create a culture of positivity, resilience, and continuous improvement. Let us always remember to honor our progress and relish each step we take towards becoming our best selves.

Core Idea 3: Finding Freedom in Flexibility

When pursuing excellence, it's essential to remember that flexibility is a powerful ally. Embracing fluidity and adaptability allows for creative solutions to emerge, enabling progress to continue unhindered by the fear of imperfection. It's crucial to recognize that rigidity can stifle innovation, whereas flexibility fosters an environment where ideas can flourish. By maintaining an open mind and a willingness to explore new approaches, we unlock the potential for breakthroughs and discoveries. This fluid mindset not only empowers individuals but also fuels collaborative efforts, as diverse perspectives can seamlessly come together to form cohesive and dynamic strategies. Moreover, in this journey towards excellence, embracing flexibility invites resilience, instilling the capacity to navigate unforeseen challenges with grace and determination. Rather than viewing deviations from initial plans as setbacks, they are reframed as opportunities to learn and recalibrate our paths towards even greater achievements. Furthermore, flexibility enables us to pivot in response to shifting landscapes, ensuring that we remain adaptable in the face of change. It fosters a culture of continuous improvement, where every twist and turn serves as a chance to grow and evolve. Ultimately, finding freedom in flexibility means choosing liberation over limitation, recognizing that the pursuit of perfection should be guided by an unwavering commitment to growth and progress, rather than a fixation on flawless outcomes. As we embrace the art of flexibility, we not only embolden ourselves to push beyond perceived boundaries but also inspire others to embrace the beauty of the imperfect journey towards greatness.

Chapter 2: The Danger of Overextending Your Resources

Core Idea 1: Embrace the Power of Prioritization

In the intricate dance of resource allocation, embracing the power of prioritization can be an absolute game-changer. Too often, organizations find themselves stretching their resources thin, attempting to be everything to everyone. It's crucial to adopt a strategic approach by identifying what's truly essential and focusing resources on those areas that align with core goals. The magic of prioritization lies in unlocking the potential for streamlined efficiency and impactful outcomes. When we prioritize effectively, we strip away the noise and hone in on what truly matters, igniting a ripple effect of productivity and success. Imagine a finely tuned orchestra, where each instrument plays its part in harmony, enhancing the overall symphony. Likewise, by prioritizing our resources, we can create a harmonious synergy within our endeavors, propelling us towards greater heights. Every resource - be it time, finances, or manpower - becomes a valuable asset dedicated to achieving significant milestones. This deliberate focus infuses every action with purpose, driving us closer to our objectives. Let's not overlook the liberating sensation that comes from shedding the unnecessary weight of non-essential tasks. Embracing prioritization empowers us to allocate our resources with intention, fostering a sense of control and mastery over our pursuits. As we harness this transformative mindset, we unlock the door to unparalleled innovation and creativity. It's the pivot towards quality over quantity, sowing the seeds for unparalleled excellence. So, let's enthusiastically embrace the power of prioritization, infusing our endeavors with intentionality and accelerating our journey towards remarkable achievement.

Core Idea 2: Finding Balance: Quality Over Quantity

In today's fast-paced world, it's easy to get caught up in the mindset of more, more, more. However, let's pause for a moment and consider the true essence of success. It's not about how much you achieve, but rather the quality of what you accomplish. Finding balance between quantity and quality is a foundational principle for sustainable growth and fulfillment.

It's tempting to fall into the trap of believing that success is synonymous with busyness or having numerous projects on the go. However, focusing on quantity alone can lead to burnout, diminished creativity, and reduced effectiveness. By prioritizing quality over quantity, we are able to give our full attention to each endeavor, allowing us to produce work of the highest caliber.

When we shift our mindset to prioritize quality, we open ourselves up to a world of possibilities. Instead of spreading ourselves thin across multiple tasks, we can devote our energy to those that truly matter. This approach enables us to pay meticulous attention to detail, infusing each project with a level of craftsmanship and excellence that cannot be achieved when our efforts are scattered.

Furthermore, by championing quality over quantity, we cultivate a reputation for delivering exceptional work. Clients and stakeholders are drawn to individuals and organizations known for consistently producing high-quality results. This distinction sets us apart in a crowded and competitive landscape, leading to greater opportunities and long-term success.

It's important to recognize that the pursuit of quality doesn't mean eschewing productivity altogether. On the contrary, by honing our focus on fewer, high-impact initiatives, we can streamline our processes, optimize our resources, and achieve remarkable efficiency. This approach empowers us to make meaningful contributions while avoiding the pitfalls of overextension and dilution of our efforts.

By embracing the philosophy of quality over quantity, we set ourselves on a path towards enduring success, personal satisfaction, and a lasting legacy. Let us strive to create works of art, projects, and endeavors that embody excellence in every sense—transformative creations that stand the test of time and elevate both ourselves and those around us.

Core Idea 3: Rejuvenate by Mastering Resource Management

When it comes to navigating the complex world of resource management, it's essential to cultivate a mindset that fosters creativity and innovation. At the heart of effective resource management lies the art of rejuvenation. True rejuvenation involves not only replenishing depleted resources but also harnessing the power of renewal to foster growth and progression. By mastering resource management, you can breathe new life into your projects and endeavors, propelling them toward success. To begin this transformative journey, it's important to acknowledge the value of diversification. Embracing diverse sources of resources can bolster your resilience and fortify your capacity to adapt to changing circumstances. Rather than relying solely on one avenue, consider exploring multiple channels to ensure a steady flow of resources, empowering your initiatives with stability and flexibility. In your pursuit of mastering resource management, it's crucial to empower yourself with the tools to assess and prioritize the allocation of resources. By embracing data-driven insights and strategic foresight, you can optimize the distribution of resources, ensuring that each facet of your endeavor receives the support it needs. Moreover, fostering a culture of collaboration and synergy among team members can spark a wave of innovation, imbuing your resource management approach with newfound vitality. Beyond the logistical aspects of resource management, it's equally important to cultivate an environment that values the holistic well-being of individuals and teams. Nurturing a spirit of mindfulness and compassion can infuse your resource management strategy with empathy and understanding, promoting resilience and sustainability. As you traverse the terrain of resource management, keep in mind that adaptability is key. Flexibility in resource allocation can unlock unforeseen potential, enabling you to seize opportunities and tackle challenges with confidence. Each resource holds inherent value, and by channeling them purposefully, you can instill your endeavors with enduring strength. Let your resource management journey be fueled by optimism and ingenuity, embracing each new day as an opportunity to flourish and thrive. By effectively rejuvenating your approach to resource management, you lay the groundwork for sustained success, inspiring those around you with the boundless possibilities that effective resource management can bring.

Chapter 3: Why Ignoring Market Research is a Costly Mistake

Core Idea 1: Discovering the Magic of Knowing Your Audience

Understanding your audience opens doors to new possibilities, fostering stronger connections and trust. When you take the time to truly understand your audience, it's like unlocking a treasure chest of opportunities. By delving into the demographics, preferences, and behaviors of your audience, you gain invaluable insights that can shape the trajectory of your success. In knowing your audience, you lay the groundwork for building meaningful connections. You can tailor your products or services to better cater to their needs, ensuring that your offerings truly resonate with them. This not only increases customer satisfaction but also boosts their trust in your brand. Moreover, understanding your audience allows you to anticipate their needs and desires, enabling you to stay ahead of the curve and provide innovative solutions. Armed with this knowledge, you can craft targeted marketing strategies that speak directly to your audience, capturing their attention and loyalty. The magic of knowing your audience resides in the transformative power it holds for your business. It opens up avenues for growth, innovation, and authenticity. Embrace the privilege of connecting on a deeper level with your audience, and watch as it propels you towards unprecedented heights of success.

Core Idea 2: Turning Insights into Exciting Opportunities

In the ever-evolving landscape of business, the ability to transform insights into boundless opportunities is an invaluable asset. As you delve into the intricate realm of market research, a treasure trove of valuable information awaits. Each nugget of data holds the potential to propel your enterprise to new heights and illuminate the path towards unprecedented success. Embracing this journey holds the promise of uncovering hidden gems that can revolutionize the way you engage with your audience.\ From understanding consumer behaviors to identifying emerging trends, every piece of the puzzle contributes to painting a vivid picture of opportunity. As you immerse yourself in the world of market research, take the time to explore the nuances of consumer desires and aspirations. By embracing empathy and insight, you'll unveil possibilities that resonate deeply with your target demographic. Armed with this profound understanding, the raw data metamorphoses into a fertile ground for cultivating innovative solutions and products that captivate your audience's imagination.\ The process of turning insights into exciting opportunities transcends mere observation; it requires the alchemy of creativity and strategic vision. This transformation breathes life into quantitative figures, as they become the catalysts for igniting fresh, exhilarating endeavors. Seizing these newfound prospects paves the way for charting unexplored territories and calibrating your trajectory for unparalleled growth. With each momentous revelation, the horizon of possibilities expands, beckoning you to embrace visionary initiatives that resonate with the pulse of your market. In this realm of abundant potential, every insight becomes an invitation to weave captivating narratives that captivate the hearts and minds of your clientele. Revel in the art of innovation as you harness the power of imagination to engineer daring ventures that hold the promise of reshaping industries and redefining paradigms. As you infuse your strategies with the vitality of these insights, the ordinary transforms into the extraordinary, and every challenge takes on the guise of an exhilarating pursuit. You stand at the precipice of a transformative journey—a journey where market research transcends mere statistics and propels you toward realms of boundless opportunity.

Core Idea 3: Empowering Growth with Data-Driven Decisions

How exhilarating it is to discover the potential for growth hidden within the treasure trove of data! In today's fast-paced business landscape, the ability to harness information and transform it into actionable insights is nothing short of miraculous. The power of data-driven decisions lies in their unwavering ability to guide us towards the most promising paths and illuminate the opportunities that align perfectly with our aspirations. Through the lens of market research and data analysis, we're able to perceive patterns, consumer behaviors, and emerging trends that might have eluded us otherwise. It's akin to embarking on a thrilling quest, armed with knowledge as our compass, to conquer new horizons and seize untold possibilities. Harnessing the wealth of information enables us to refine our strategies, innovate with confidence, and adventure into uncharted territories. Embracing a data-driven approach empowers us to make informed decisions that propel our organizations towards unprecedented success. As we navigate through the ever-changing marketplace, we wield the strength of data as our guiding light, thwarting uncertainty and doubt with every step we take. Every data point becomes a beacon of hope, illuminating the way forward and reassuring us that our choices are not left to chance. In this dawning era of digital transformation, data stands as the foundation upon which monumental achievements are built. No longer do we rely solely on intuition or speculation; instead, we embrace the precision and reliability of insights derived from data analysis. With each decision fortified by data, we stand emboldened to take bold strides towards our goals, unfazed by the unknown and undeterred by challenges. So let us celebrate the marvels of data-driven decisions, for they are the catalysts that ignite our journey towards greatness and infuse every endeavor with boundless promise.

Chapter 4: Steering Away from Micromanagement

Core Idea 1: Embracing the Art of Delegation

Delegation is not just a means to distribute tasks, but an art form that enables us to make the most of our resources. It allows us to prioritize our focus on strategic goals, while empowering and entrusting others to take ownership of specific responsibilities. Embracing the art of delegation does not imply relinquishing control; rather, it signals a shift towards a more evolved leadership style where trust and collaboration thrive. By delegating effectively, we create a ripple effect within our teams, fostering a culture of empowerment and accountability. As leaders, embracing delegation signals our commitment to nurturing talent and unlocking the full potential of our team members. It's about recognizing and harnessing the unique skills and strengths of individuals, enabling them to contribute meaningfully to the collective success. Furthermore, by sharing the workload, we pave the way for innovation and creativity to flourish, as individuals feel empowered to explore new approaches and solutions. In doing so, we build a resilient and agile organization that can adapt to change and thrive in dynamic environments. Embracing delegation elevates the entire team, lifting morale and fostering a sense of unity and purpose. When each team member feels entrusted with meaningful responsibility, they are more invested in the outcomes, driving a shared commitment to excellence. Ultimately, by embracing the art of delegation, we cultivate a culture of mutual support, growth, and accomplishment, where every individual has the opportunity to shine and contribute to the broader vision.

Core Idea 2: Fostering an Empowered Team Environment

In the quest for sustained success, fostering an empowered team environment is a pivotal component that drives motivation, innovation, and ultimately, productivity within your organization. As a leader, it's paramount to recognize the immense potential that lies within each member of your team and to provide them with the autonomy and trust necessary to flourish. Empowerment encompasses more than just delegation; it is about instilling a sense of ownership and accountability, creating a culture where individuals feel valued and capable of making meaningful contributions. By nurturing a collaborative atmosphere where voices are heard, ideas are championed, and creativity is encouraged, you equip your team members to unleash their full potential. Open lines of communication and transparent decision-making processes form the cornerstone of an empowered environment, promoting inclusivity and fostering a shared vision. This environment gives rise to a collective spirit that propels forward momentum, ignites passion, and cultivates a sense of purpose among team members. Embracing diversity in thought and approach further enriches the tapestry of ideas, leading to innovative solutions and transformative outcomes. Recognizing and celebrating individual and collective achievements within an empowered team environment strengthens morale, bolsters confidence, and fuels an enduring commitment to excellence. Moreover, providing opportunities for professional growth, skill development, and continuous learning underscores your dedication to nurturing a culture of empowerment. When each team member feels empowered to contribute, take initiative, and embrace challenges with resilience, the ripple effect is transformative, leading to elevated engagement and a dynamic, high-performing team.

Fostering an empowered team environment is not simply a strategy—it is a philosophy, a mindset, and a catalyst for sustainable success.

Core Idea 3: Cultivating Trust and Celebrating Independence

Creating a work environment where trust flourishes is a cornerstone of effective leadership. When leaders foster an atmosphere of trust, they empower their team members to thrive in an environment that celebrates independence. Building trust involves open communication, transparency, and consistency. Communicate clearly and openly with your team to keep them informed about the organization's goals, strategies, and expectations. Transparency not only promotes trust but also encourages team members to share their ideas and concerns without fear. Consistency in decision-making and action establishes a sense of reliability and predictability, instilling confidence in the team.

Recognizing and celebrating independence within the team is equally important. Encouraging autonomy and allowing individuals to make decisions fosters a sense of ownership and responsibility. Provide opportunities for team members to take the lead on projects, make decisions, and showcase their unique talents. By doing so, you create an environment where innovation and creativity can flourish. Acknowledge and appreciate the contributions of each team member, valuing the diverse perspectives and skills they bring to the table. This not only fuels individual growth but also strengthens the collective bond of the team.

As a leader, it is essential to establish a culture that respects individual autonomy while promoting collaboration. Embrace a leadership style that supports and guides rather than micromanages. Empower your team through mentorship and coaching, providing them with the necessary tools and resources to excel. Encourage open dialogue and feedback loops to nurture a culture of continuous improvement. When trust and independence are celebrated, team members feel empowered to step into their full potential, fostering a vibrant and dynamic work environment.

By cultivating trust and celebrating independence, leaders lay the foundation for a high-performing, motivated, and engaged team. Team members feel valued, respected, and trusted, resulting in increased morale, productivity, and overall job satisfaction. A culture of trust and independence breeds loyalty and commitment, leading to a cohesive and harmonious work environment where everyone can contribute their best. As a leader, embody the values of trust and independence, and watch as your team rises to surpass expectations and achieve remarkable success.

Chapter 5: Don't Underestimate the Power of a Plan

Core Idea 1: The Foundation of Dreams: Building a Visionary Blueprint

A clear vision sets the direction and fuels motivation, providing a roadmap to guide decisions and actions. When we dare to dream and envision the future we desire, we lay the foundation for something extraordinary. It's in the realm of our dreams that we sow the seeds of innovation and progress, igniting our passion and purpose. Through crafting a visionary blueprint, we have the power to harness the limitless potential within us. This process empowers us to define our aspirations clearly, allowing us to set meaningful goals and objectives. The visionary blueprint becomes our guiding light, illuminating possibilities and steering us toward unprecedented achievements. With each stroke of imagination and foresight, we breathe life into our ambitions, transforming them from mere ideas into tangible realities. As we refine and shape our visionary blueprint, we infuse it with our unwavering belief in what is possible. This clarity not only propels us forward but also inspires and influences those around us. It fosters a sense of unity and collective purpose, aligning individuals and teams toward a common goal. Moreover, the visionary blueprint acts as a constant reminder of the heights we seek to reach, instilling resilience and perseverance during moments of challenge or adversity. Embracing this foundational step propels us toward a future brimming with boundless opportunities and transformative accomplishments.

Core Idea 2: Transforming Ideas into Action: Crafting Your Path to Success

Once the visionary blueprint is in place, it's time to transform those brilliant ideas into tangible actions. This is the phase where dreams take flight and aspirations turn into exhilarating realities. To begin with, identify the pivotal steps required to propel your vision forward. Break down each component into manageable tasks, establishing a clear roadmap that leads to triumph.

Embracing the power of proactivity is essential during this phase of transformation. While envisioning the future is crucial, taking decisive actions accelerates progress and fosters momentum. Allow your enthusiasm and determination to ignite the pursuit of your goals, infusing every step with passion and purpose.

Crafting your path to success involves nurturing an unwavering belief in your capabilities and the boundless potential of your vision. Embrace each challenge as an opportunity for growth, knowing that every obstacle conquered brings you closer to your ultimate destination. Harness the energy within yourself and those around you to manifest a reality that surpasses even your most audacious dreams.

Remember, the pathway to success is not always linear; it may twist and turn, presenting unexpected opportunities and unforeseen hurdles. Embracing adaptability allows you to navigate through these fluctuations with grace and resilience. Stay agile in your approach, reassessing and adjusting your course as necessary while remaining steadfast in your commitment to realizing your aspirations.

As you forge ahead, incorporate flexibility into your strategies, enabling fluidity that harmonizes with the evolving landscape of your journey. Transforming ideas into action requires an unwavering dedication to continuous improvement, a willingness to absorb lessons from both victories and defeats, and an enduring spirit that thrives amidst uncertainty.

Ultimately, crafting your path to success is an art form, a symphony of ambition, grit, and unwavering optimism. Embody the essence of determination, infuse each action with purpose, and radiate the unyielding belief that your vision will not only come to fruition but will thrive in ways beyond your wildest imagination.

Core Idea 3: Embracing Adaptability: Growing and Evolving with Purpose

In the journey of turning our dreams into reality, adaptability plays a pivotal role. It is the art of embracing change and evolving with purpose that propels us forward on the path to success. As we navigate the ever-changing landscape of opportunities and challenges, understanding the need to adapt becomes imperative. Embracing adaptability empowers us to innovate, learn from experiences, and expand our horizons. It's about being open to new ideas, insights, and perspectives, without losing sight of our core values and goals.

Adaptability enables us to seamlessly pivot and recalibrate our strategies when faced with unexpected changes. By approaching unforeseen circumstances with resilience and flexibility, we can transform setbacks into opportunities for growth. This mindset allows us to remain proactive, rather than reactive, in the face of adversity. Moreover, it fosters a culture of creativity and continuous improvement within our professional and personal endeavors.

As we embrace adaptability, we not only respond to challenges but also proactively seek out new avenues for advancement. This proactive approach enables us to anticipate shifts in the market, industry trends, and customer needs, positioning us ahead of the curve. By remaining agile and adaptive, we create an environment where innovation thrives and where we can harness change as a catalyst for progress.

Additionally, adopting an adaptable mindset fosters a spirit of collaboration and empowerment within teams and organizations. When individuals are receptive to change, they contribute diverse perspectives and readily support each other through transitions. This collective adaptability forms a foundation for cohesive teamwork, resourcefulness, and united problem-solving, ultimately leading to higher levels of achievement and fulfillment.

Embracing adaptability also encourages continual learning and self-improvement. It cultivates a growth mindset, driving us to seek knowledge, refine our skills, and explore new possibilities. Through this ongoing evolution, we unlock untapped potential within ourselves and inspire others to embark on their own transformative journeys.

In conclusion, embracing adaptability is not just about surviving in an ever-changing world; it's about thriving and leading with purpose. It is a conscious choice that empowers us to navigate complexities, seize opportunities, and drive meaningful progress. By embodying adaptability, we set the stage for transformative growth and lay the groundwork for a future defined by innovation, resilience, and purposeful evolution.

Chapter 6: The Importance of Embracing Technology

Core Idea 1: Harnessing the Power of Progress: A Journey into Modern Tools

In today's fast-paced world, the landscape of business and innovation is constantly evolving. It is crucial to embrace the power of progress by harnessing the potential of modern tools. As we journey into the realm of contemporary technologies, we are presented with an array of resources that have the capacity to propel our vision forward and drive transformative change within our organizations. By exploring the latest innovations in technology, we open doors to unlocking unprecedented opportunities and unleashing the full potential of our endeavors. Through the integration of cutting-edge solutions, we can enhance productivity, streamline processes, and foster a culture of innovation and adaptability. Embracing modern tools allows us to stay ahead of the curve, positioning ourselves as pioneers in our respective industries. The fusion of visionary leadership and technological advancements lays the groundwork for pioneering initiatives that redefine standards and revolutionize operations. This journey into modern tools is not just a quest for efficiency, but a pursuit of excellence. It's about embracing the spirit of progress and leveraging the boundless capabilities that technology offers. By wholeheartedly embracing this journey, we embark on a path toward sustainable growth, strategic differentiation, and enduring success. Let us seize this moment to champion the cause of progress and leverage the transformative power of modern tools in shaping a future where innovation knows no bounds.

Core Idea 2: Digital Transformations: Unlocking New Horizons

In today's fast-paced world, the digital landscape is continually evolving, presenting us with unprecedented opportunities to revolutionize our approach to business. Embracing digital transformations not only propels us into the future but also unlocks new horizons of possibility and potential. From sophisticated data analytics to immersive virtual reality experiences, the realm of technology offers a canvas on which we can paint the masterpiece of tomorrow. Through cloud computing, businesses of any size can now access powerful tools and resources that were once reserved for industry giants. This democratization of technology empowers entrepreneurs and innovators to manifest their visions without the constraints of traditional barriers. It's a thrilling era where bold ideas are transformed into tangible reality through the fusion of creativity and technology. As we navigate this digital frontier, it's essential to cultivate a mindset of adaptability and curiosity. Rather than fearing change, let's embrace it as an opportunity for growth and expansion. By understanding the transformative potential of technology, we open ourselves to unconventional solutions and groundbreaking innovation. The integration of artificial intelligence and machine learning has the potential to amplify our productivity and efficiency, allowing us to focus on what truly matters – creating value for our customers and stakeholders. Moreover, the interconnectedness of the digital age has dissolved geographical boundaries, connecting us with a global network of minds and talents. This interconnectedness fosters collaboration and knowledge-sharing, sparking a renaissance of collective progress. In essence, digital transformation isn't merely about adopting the latest gadgets or software; it's about infusing every aspect of our operations with a spirit of limitless possibilities. It's about daring to dream big and leveraging technology to turn those dreams into reality. With each technological leap, we stand on the precipice of a new horizon, ready to seize the untold opportunities that await us.

Core Idea 3: Building Bridges to Tomorrow Through Innovation

In today's rapidly evolving business landscape, innovation stands as the cornerstone of progress and success. As we delve into the realm of embracing technology, it becomes abundantly clear that building bridges to tomorrow is not only crucial but also exhilarating. Innovation paves the way for businesses to surpass their own limits and propel themselves into new realms of possibility. It is the force that fuels transformation and fosters an environment of perpetual evolution. Embracing technological innovation means actively engaging with change, adapting strategies, and envisioning a future that transcends current limitations. This forward-looking approach ensures that your business stays at the forefront of development, continuously evolving and surpassing itself in remarkable ways. Through embracing innovation, you're not merely adapting to the times; you're orchestrating the very orchestration of change, creating ripples of progress that extend far beyond the present moment. It's about weaving a narrative of continual growth, where each technological advancement isn't just a tool, but a stepping stone towards a brighter, more prosperous future. We must remember that innovation isn't confined to technological advancements alone. True innovation encompasses a mindset, a relentless pursuit of improvement and a willingness to break free from conventional boundaries. By fostering a culture of innovation within your organization, you encourage bold ideas to flourish, creating an ecosystem where imagination thrives and possibilities are endless. With this spirit of innovation driving us, we become architects of the future, constructing pathways that lead to uncharted territories of success. Each stride we take, fueled by our commitment to embracing technology, becomes a testament to our determination to shape a future that outshines even our most audacious visions. It's a journey rife with rewards, as we witness our efforts culminate in solutions that revolutionize industries and empower communities. So, let us embrace technology not just as a tool, but as a catalyst for transformation – for in doing so, we embark on a journey that doesn't just span lifetimes, but reshapes them.

Chapter 7: Navigating the Minefield of Poor Financial Planning

Core Idea 01: Building a Bright Financial Future: Understand and Embrace the Basics

Understanding financial fundamentals lays the groundwork for prosperous growth. Building a bright financial future starts with a deep understanding of the basic principles that underpin sound financial planning. It's akin to constructing a sturdy foundation for a home–without it, the entire structure may become unstable. By embracing the basics, individuals can pave the way for lasting prosperity. First and foremost, it's crucial to comprehend the concept of budgeting and how it plays a pivotal role in managing personal or business finances. Budgeting empowers individuals to allocate resources wisely, avoid unnecessary expenses, and develop a financial cushion for unforeseen circumstances. Moreover, understanding the importance of saving and investing allows for the growth and preservation of wealth. The art of diversification and risk management should not be overlooked as it ensures a resilient financial portfolio. Embracing the power of compounding interest and its potential to multiply wealth over time is also essential. Finally, fostering a mindset of financial literacy and continuous learning sets the stage for making informed and calculated financial decisions. As individuals and businesses gain proficiency in these fundamental concepts, a brighter financial future comes into focus, filled with opportunities and security.

Core Idea 2: Strategize Your Wealth: Develop Empowering Budgets and Forecasts

Developing empowering budgets and forecasts is a crucial step in steering your financial ship towards success. It's not just about tracking your expenses and income; it's about crafting a roadmap that guides you towards your desired financial destination. As you embark on this journey, remember to embrace the process with optimism and enthusiasm. Building a bright financial future starts with clear, actionable plans and the determination to see them through. When creating budgets, view them as tools for empowerment rather than constraints. They are the building blocks of your financial freedom, providing a solid structure upon which you can grow and thrive. Think of them as the seeds from which your wealth will blossom. While budgets enable you to track your progress, forecasts allow you to chart your future course. By envisioning where you want to be, you are empowering yourself to make decisions today that will lead to tomorrow's successes. Embrace the power of visualization and strategic planning - picture your ideal financial landscape and use that image as fuel for your actions. Consider your forecasts as a canvas on which you paint the vibrant portrait of your financial dreams. This process isn't about restriction; it's about liberation. It's about designing a life of abundance, where your resources are aligned with your aspirations. Embrace the opportunities that come with managing your finances wisely. See each budget line as an avenue for nurturing your goals and aspirations. Your allowance for savings isn't a sacrifice; it's a tribute to your future. Your investment strategy isn't a burden; it's a celebration of growth and opportunity. Through budgets and forecasts, you are sculpting a path that leads to financial empowerment - a path that allows you to realize your dreams and live a life of abundance. Keep your spirit high as you delve into this aspect of financial planning. It's not just about numbers and spreadsheets; it's about crafting a narrative of prosperity. Embrace the journey, knowing that each step brings you closer to the financial success you deserve.

Core Idea 3: Unlocking Potential: Leverage Tools and Resources for Financial Success

As you embark on your journey to financial success, it's important to recognize that you have an array of tools and resources at your disposal. These resources can serve as powerful allies in your pursuit of prosperity, helping you navigate the intricate landscape of finance with confidence and competence.

One of the most valuable resources available to you is knowledge. Educate yourself about different investment opportunities, financial instruments, and strategies for wealth accumulation. Stay informed about market trends and economic indicators, and use this knowledge to make informed decisions that align with your long-term objectives.

In addition to knowledge, technological innovations present an abundance of resources that can streamline your financial management. Embrace the power of financial software and digital platforms that enable you to track expenses, monitor investments, and analyze market data in real time. By leveraging such tools, you can gain unparalleled insights into your financial standing and make swift, well-informed decisions to optimize your assets.

Beyond technology, don't underestimate the importance of networking and seeking guidance from financial experts. Establish connections with experienced professionals who can provide valuable advice tailored to your specific goals and circumstances. Whether it's consulting with a seasoned financial advisor, engaging in mentorship programs, or participating in industry events, surrounding yourself with knowledgeable individuals can broaden your perspective and open doors to new opportunities.

Furthermore, consider exploring alternative investment vehicles and diversifying your portfolio to harness the potential for greater returns. From real estate to venture capital, don't confine yourself to traditional avenues; instead, explore innovative options that align with your risk tolerance and long-term aspirations.

Remember, the key to leveraging these tools and resources lies in active engagement and continuous learning. Stay curious, remain adaptable, and view each new resource as a stepping stone toward your financial ambitions. By harnessing the potential inherent in these resources, you'll empower yourself to navigate the realm of finance with resilience, creativity, and unwavering optimism.

Chapter 8: Avoiding Neglect of Customer Relationships

Core Idea 1: Embracing the Joy of Connection

In today's fast-paced and interconnected world, the value of genuine human connection cannot be overstated. When it comes to business, building and nurturing meaningful relationships with customers is pivotal in establishing a loyal and satisfied customer base. It goes beyond transactional interactions; it's about creating emotional bonds and fostering a sense of belonging. Embracing the joy of connection means recognizing the humanity in every individual customer. It involves actively listening to their needs, understanding their preferences, and empathizing with their challenges. By doing so, businesses can cultivate trust and demonstrate that they genuinely care. This bond of trust forms the foundation for long-lasting relationships, paving the way for continued patronage and enthusiastic referrals. Moreover, embracing the joy of connection allows businesses to tailor their products or services to better cater to their customers' specific desires and aspirations. This personalization shows customers that they are valued as individuals, not just as buyers. When customers feel understood and appreciated, they become more than just patrons – they become advocates for the brand. Their positive experiences and emotional connections lead to organic word-of-mouth marketing, which is incredibly powerful in today's digital landscape. People are drawn to authentic and uplifting interactions, and by embracing the joy of connection, businesses can create memorable experiences that resonate deeply with customers. In turn, this fosters an environment of continuous improvement and innovation as businesses strive to exceed customer expectations. Ultimately, the joy of connection leads to a virtuous cycle of mutual growth, where both businesses and customers thrive in harmony.

Core Idea 2: Building Lasting Bridges of Trust

In our journey to business success, it's essential to recognize the critical role that trust plays in nurturing and solidifying customer relationships. Building lasting bridges of trust goes beyond transactions; it embodies the spirit of authenticity, reliability, and a genuine commitment to mutual growth.

Trust is the cornerstone of any enduring relationship. It forms the bedrock on which fruitful collaborations, partnerships, and long-term associations are built. For businesses, earning this trust means living up to promises, consistently delivering value, and maintaining open lines of communication. Customers need to feel confident that their needs and concerns are valued and will be addressed with sincerity and empathy.

One powerful tool for building bridges of trust is transparency. By being open and honest about our processes, products, and services, we demonstrate respect for our customers' intelligence and their right to make informed decisions. Transparency breeds confidence and fosters a sense of partnership, leading to deeper connections and loyalty.

Moreover, fostering trust involves actively listening to our customers. When they share their feedback, suggestions, or even grievances, embracing an attitude of openness and attentiveness can turn a potential challenge into an opportunity for growth. Taking the time to understand their perspectives and demonstrating a genuine willingness to address their concerns reinforces the foundation of trust and builds a strong emotional connection.

It's equally important to acknowledge the power of consistency in building lasting bridges of trust. Consistency in product quality, service excellence, and brand messaging creates a sense of dependability that resonates with customers. When they know what to expect from us and we deliver on those expectations time and again, a profound sense of reliability and trust begins to take root.

The concept of reciprocity also plays a significant role in building bridges of trust. When we demonstrate our commitment to the well-being and success of our customers, without solely focusing on our gains, we sow the seeds for a strong and enduring partnership. When customers feel genuinely cared for and supported, they are more likely to reciprocate with loyalty and advocacy.

The process of building lasting bridges of trust is multifaceted, encompassing transparency, active listening, consistency, and a genuine spirit of reciprocity. As we navigate this path, let's embrace the uplifting realization that each bridge we build adds strength not only to our business but also to the lives and experiences of those we serve.

Core Idea 3: Nurturing Relationships for Mutual Growth

In the wonderful tapestry of business, nurturing relationships is akin to tending a beautiful garden. Just as a gardener lovingly tends to each plant for it to flourish, entrepreneurs and business leaders must likewise invest time and effort into nurturing their relationships for mutual growth. Building and maintaining fruitful connections with clients, partners, and stakeholders is not merely a transactional endeavor, but a deeply enriching journey of trust, empathy, and collaboration.

Nurturing relationships for mutual growth entails recognizing and celebrating the uniqueness of each connection. It involves understanding that a successful partnership is a harmonious dance of two entities, each bringing their distinct strengths to the table. This process requires a genuine interest in the well-being and success of the other party, beyond immediate gains. By fostering an environment of mutual respect and support, relationships can transcend the mundane and evolve into enduring sources of inspiration and innovation.

One of the most powerful ways to nurture relationships is through active listening and thoughtful communication. Taking the time to truly understand the needs and aspirations of your business associates fosters a culture of empathy and understanding. This, in turn, strengthens the bonds of trust and lays the foundation for collaborative achievements. Each interaction becomes an opportunity to sow the seeds of goodwill and reciprocity, cultivating an atmosphere where both parties feel valued and validated.

Moreover, nurturing relationships for mutual growth involves a willingness to offer support and mentorship. As you seek to uplift others and help them thrive, you inevitably create ripples of positivity that reverberate back to enhance your own growth and development. By being a source of encouragement and insight, you become an invaluable partner on the shared path towards success, fostering an ecosystem of reciprocity and abundance.

Finally, the cultivation of relationships for mutual growth thrives on transparency and integrity. Open and honest communication, combined with ethical conduct, forms the bedrock of enduring, symbiotic relationships. When trust is placed at the forefront of every interaction, it breeds an environment of dependability and assurance, paving the way for long-term collaborative ventures and shared triumphs.

In conclusion, nurturing relationships for mutual growth is a testament to the transformative power of genuine connections. By investing in the holistic well-being and progress of those around us, we weave a tapestry of interconnected successes that elevate both parties. It is through this uplifting journey of mutual growth that we cultivate a landscape where prosperity, creativity, and fulfillment bloom abundantly, enriching every facet of our professional endeavors.

Chapter 9: The Perils of Stagnation and Resistance to Change

Core Idea 1: Embracing Change as a Catalyst for Growth

Change, often synonymous with growth and evolution, has the remarkable power to propel individuals, businesses, and industries towards new heights of success. Embracing change is akin to opening the door to endless possibilities and opportunities, paving the way for innovation and advancement. The beauty of change lies in its ability to reshape perspectives, breathe new life into endeavors, and inspire individuals to reach beyond their perceived limitations.

When we explore inspiring stories of transformation, we uncover a tapestry woven from the threads of courage, resilience, and the unwavering spirit to embrace change. From humble beginnings to meteoric success, these narratives epitomize the profound impact of adapting to change. They serve as beacons of hope and motivation, shining a light on the incredible outcomes that await those who dare to embrace change with open arms.

One such story revolves around a small start-up that weathered numerous storms in its infancy. Instead of succumbing to adversity, the visionary leaders collectively decided to pivot their approach, aligning with changing market dynamics. With unyielding dedication and an embracing mindset, they transformed their obstacles into stepping stones, ultimately achieving unprecedented feats that surpassed their wildest dreams. This is the story of what our business did in our beginnings and our pivot in the midst of the COVID pandemic when we repurposed a restaurant into a delivery grocery and liquor store. This account reflects the transformative power of change and acts as a testament to the immense potential nestled within its folds.

Moreover, delving into the realm of personal growth unravels countless anecdotes of individuals who championed change fearlessly. These individuals recognized that embarking on the journey of self-improvement demanded a willingness to adapt and evolve continually. Stepping out of their comfort zones, they prioritized learning, honed new skills, and welcomed change as an ever-present companion on their quest for personal and professional fulfillment.

By bringing these uplifting narratives to the forefront, we gain valuable insights into the capacity of change to generate growth and catalyze progress. These stories serve as guiding stars, illuminating the path to realizing our potential and redefining what is achievable. In embracing change as a catalyst for growth, we not only embark on a transformative journey but also sow the seeds for a future brimming with promise, optimism, and unparalleled success.

Core Idea 2: Cultivating an Adaptable Mindset

A crucial element in navigating the tumultuous waters of change and transformation is cultivating an adaptable mindset. By fostering a mentality that embraces flexibility and nimbleness, individuals and organizations can thrive amidst uncertainty. This adaptable mindset starts with acknowledging that change is inevitable and that our responses to it shape our outcomes. Rather than resisting change out of fear or clinging to outdated methods, individuals who cultivate adaptability approach new situations with curiosity and open-mindedness. They understand that each shift brings opportunities for growth and innovation. Cultivating an adaptable mindset also involves developing resilience—viewing setbacks as temporary and learning experiences as opportunities for self-improvement. It's about reframing challenges as stepping stones to success rather than insurmountable obstacles. Embracing an adaptable mindset also requires an ongoing commitment to continuous learning and skill development. This involves staying abreast of industry trends, seeking out new knowledge, and honing one's abilities to meet the demands of a rapidly evolving landscape. Moreover, those with an adaptable mindset see change not as something to be feared, but as something to be leveraged for personal and professional development. They embrace uncertainty as an invitation to push boundaries, experiment, and uncover new solutions. By approaching change with optimism and a growth-oriented perspective, individuals can transform challenges into opportunities and drive meaningful progress. Importantly, cultivating an adaptable mindset is not just a personal endeavor—it's a cultural and organizational imperative. Leaders play a pivotal role in setting the tone for adaptability within their teams and fostering an environment where flexibility and agility are celebrated. By championing a culture that rewards innovation, risk-taking, and learning from failure, they inspire their teams to embrace change with confidence rather than trepidation. In doing so, they foster an atmosphere where creativity flourishes, collaboration thrives, and forward-thinking solutions emerge. Cultivating an adaptable mindset isn't merely about weathering storms; it's about harnessing the winds of change to soar to new heights. Through the resilience, curiosity, and learning that define this mindset, individuals and organizations not only survive in times of upheaval, but they emerge stronger, more agile, and better equipped to seize new opportunities on the horizon.

Core Idea 3: Celebrating the Journey of Transformation

Transformation is a beautiful and awe-inspiring process that unfolds before us, marking the evolution of individuals and organizations alike. As we navigate through the ever-changing landscapes of our lives and work, it's crucial to recognize and celebrate each step taken towards positive metamorphosis. The journey of transformation is not merely a linear progression, but rather a tapestry of experiences, learnings, and growth.

At the heart of celebrating transformation lies the acknowledgment of resilience and adaptability. When faced with challenges and obstacles, it's our ability to embrace change, pivot when necessary, and boldly venture into uncharted territories that truly defines our transformative capacity. By commemorating the spirit of adaptability, we honor the courage it takes to step outside comfort zones and embrace new possibilities, propelling ourselves towards unforeseen heights.

Moreover, celebrating transformation entails acknowledging the collective efforts and collaborative energies that pave the way for innovation and progress. It's about recognizing the contributions of every individual involved, fostering an environment where diverse perspectives converge, and creating a shared vision for the future. Through this celebration, we weave a narrative of unity and synergy, amplifying the impact of transformation and ensuring that no voice or effort goes unnoticed. It's a joyous ode to teamwork, solidarity, and the power of collective transformation.

As we traverse the path of transformation, it's equally important to celebrate the small victories along the way. Each milestone achieved, every lesson learned, and every instance of growth warrants acknowledgement and celebration. These moments of triumph serve as beacons of inspiration, igniting a flame of optimism within us and reaffirming our belief in the potential for continual improvement and evolution.

Ultimately, celebrating the journey of transformation is about embracing gratitude for the opportunities presented by change. It's a testament to the unwavering belief in the potential for positive change, and an expression of thankfulness for the wisdom gained through each transformative experience. By reveling in the process of transformation, we infuse our endeavors with a sense of purpose and passion, fostering an environment where change is not feared, but welcomed as a catalyst for boundless growth and renewal.

Chapter 10: Sidestepping Ineffective Team Management

Core Idea 1: Fostering a Culture of Collaboration and Trust

Encouraging open communication and providing platforms for team members to express their ideas freely are crucial steps in fostering a culture of collaboration and trust within any organization. When team members feel that their input is valued and actively sought after, they are more likely to engage fully in the team's goals and objectives. By creating an environment where every voice is heard and respected, leaders can cultivate a sense of belonging and inclusivity. This inclusivity breeds creativity, as diverse perspectives fuel innovation and problem-solving. Moreover, when team members feel empowered to share their thoughts and insights, it strengthens their commitment to the team's mission and enhances their sense of ownership. A transparent and inclusive atmosphere builds trust, leading to higher morale and job satisfaction among team members. As teams collaborate more effectively, they become stronger and more resilient. In turn, this fosters an environment in which individuals are comfortable taking risks and exploring new ideas, knowing that the team will support and learn from both successes and challenges. Encouraging collaboration also provides opportunities for mentorship and the sharing of knowledge and skills. As team members work together towards shared goals, they develop a deeper understanding of each other's strengths and contributions, building a more cohesive and supportive work environment. Overall, by nurturing a culture of collaboration and trust, leaders empower their teams to achieve remarkable results while fostering a sense of unity and camaraderie.

Core Idea2: Empowering Leadership: Guiding with Inspiration

Effective leadership is not just about giving orders or making decisions; it's about inspiring and guiding your team to achieve greatness. Empowering leadership goes beyond traditional methods of management and instead focuses on fostering a sense of purpose and drive within each team member. It's about leading by example, showing empathy, and creating an environment where everyone feels supported and motivated. When you embrace empowering leadership, you tap into the potential of your team, unleashing their creativity and resourcefulness. By cultivating a culture of empowerment, you allow each individual to contribute their unique strengths and ideas, leading to greater innovation and success. As a leader, your role is to provide guidance and support, not to micro-manage every task. Trusting your team members to make decisions and take ownership of their work not only boosts their confidence but also builds a sense of accountability. This approach fosters a dynamic and collaborative atmosphere, where everyone feels valued and appreciated. Empowering leadership also involves recognizing and nurturing talents within your team. By acknowledging each person's abilities and encouraging them to develop their skills, you create a space for personal and professional growth. Encouraging continuous learning and skill development not only benefits the individual but also strengthens the overall capabilities of the team. Moreover, as a leader, your enthusiasm and positivity can set the tone for the entire team. By maintaining a hopeful and confident outlook, you inspire others to tackle challenges with resilience and determination. Your belief in the team's potential becomes contagious, motivating everyone to strive for excellence. Ultimately, empowering leadership is about creating a harmonious and energizing environment where each team member feels empowered to contribute their best. When leaders guide with inspiration, they pave the way for breakthroughs, collaboration, and collective success. This type of leadership is transformative, shaping not only the present but also the future of the team and the organization. As you cultivate an environment of empowerment, you'll witness your team thrive and surpass expectations, attaining achievements that seemed unattainable before.

Core Idea 3: Celebrating Collective Success and Learning from Challenges

Success and challenges are two sides of the same coin, each offering invaluable lessons and opportunities for growth. In cultivating effective team management, it's crucial to create a culture that celebrates collective success and embraces challenges as stepping stones to greatness. By acknowledging and celebrating the accomplishments of the team as a whole, you foster a sense of unity and shared purpose. This can bolster morale, reinforcing the idea that every individual plays an integral part in the team's achievements. Recognizing and embracing challenges also fuels a culture of resilience and innovation. When faced with obstacles, teams that approach challenges as opportunities for learning and improvement are better positioned to emerge stronger and more cohesive. Sharing stories of overcoming adversity can inspire and motivate team members, fostering a mindset of determination and perseverance. It's important to create platforms for team members to share their experiences, both positive and challenging, allowing others to learn from their journeys. Additionally, establishing rituals or events that commemorate milestones and showcase the journey taken by the team can further solidify a sense of unity and common purpose. Through these celebrations, team members can reflect on past successes, reinforcing the belief in the team's potential and creating a collective memory of triumphs. Reflecting on challenges also provides an opportunity for introspection and growth. Encouraging open discussions about past setbacks and the lessons learned helps teams evolve and adapt. It fosters a culture of continuous improvement and resilience, where failures are reframed as valuable learning experiences. Moreover, emphasizing the importance of learning from challenges can stimulate creative problem-solving and innovative thinking within the team. Individuals are more likely to approach obstacles with creativity and resourcefulness when they perceive them as opportunities for growth rather than insurmountable barriers. Celebrating collective success and learning from challenges not only strengthens the fabric of the team but also encourages a forward-looking and optimistic approach to future endeavors. It reinforces the idea that success is a shared experience, and challenges are merely temporary roadblocks on the path to greater achievements. Building a team culture rooted in celebration and resilience paves the way for sustained success and enduring camaraderie.

Chapter 11: Action Steps: Crafting Your Success Story

Core Action 1: Reflecting on the Journey: Celebrating Milestones

As we embark on the exhilarating journey of crafting our success story, it is essential to pause and bask in the rays of our achievements. Each milestone serves as a glittering gem in the tapestry of our progress, signifying our unwavering dedication and persistence. Cast your mind back to the genesis of your endeavors, where dreams were mere sparks in the darkness of uncertainty. Recall the pivotal moments that illuminated your path, paving the way for growth and triumph. Whether it was securing your first client, overcoming a daunting challenge, or reaching a significant financial goal, each victory holds significance and deserves recognition. These milestones are not merely markers of progress but treasures that embody the essence of your perseverance and resilience. By celebrating them, we honor the sheer determination that propels us forward amidst the trials and tribulations. Take a moment to cherish these stepping stones, for they have fortified the bedrock upon which your remarkable journey has been constructed. Let gratitude fill your heart as you acknowledge the countless hours of hard work, the sacrifices made, and the lessons learned. Reflecting on the journey elevates our spirits, providing an opportunity to draw inspiration from our past accomplishments and infuse our future endeavors with renewed vigor. It reinforces our belief in our capabilities, serving as a testament to our ability to conquer challenges and emerge triumphant. In embracing these milestones, we derive the strength to propel ourselves towards even greater heights, armed with the wisdom gleaned from our experiences. So, let us celebrate the courage, tenacity, and determination that have brought us this far and brace ourselves for the extraordinary chapters that await in our continued pursuit of success.

Core Action 2: Empowering Forward Motion: Building a Roadmap to Continued Success

As we look back on the journey that has brought us to this point, it's essential to find inspiration in the milestones we've achieved. However, it's equally crucial to focus on the path ahead, charting a course for continued growth and prosperity. Crafting your success story requires a deliberate and strategic approach, one that empowers forward motion and promotes sustained achievement. It begins with creating a comprehensive roadmap that not only acknowledges past triumphs but also paves the way for future accomplishments. The first step in building this roadmap is envisioning your ultimate destination. What does success look like for you, both personally and professionally? By painting a vivid picture of the future you wish to create, you lay the foundation for meaningful and purposeful actions. Next, consider the milestones and objectives that will mark your progress along the way. These should be specific, measurable, achievable, relevant, and time-bound (SMART). Cleary defined goals provide direction and serve as checkpoints on your journey, ensuring you stay on track and can celebrate incremental victories. A critical aspect of this roadmap to continued success involves the identification of potential obstacles and challenges. By acknowledging these potential roadblocks, you can prepare contingency plans and develop resilience strategies. Additionally, seeking support from mentors, peers, or industry experts can provide valuable insights and guidance, helping mitigate risks and overcome hurdles. Embracing flexibility is another key component of crafting a forward-focused roadmap. While having a clear vision is important, it's equally vital to remain adaptable in response to unforeseen opportunities or shifts in the business landscape. Embracing change as an opportunity for growth can unlock new pathways to success and innovation. Finally, no roadmap to continued success would be complete without a commitment to ongoing learning and development. Embracing a mindset of continuous improvement fosters creativity and adaption to emerging trends, ensuring your success story remains vibrant and dynamic. By embodying these principles and constructing a strategic roadmap, you can empower forward motion toward sustained success, poised to embrace the future with optimism and resilience.

Core Action 3: Embracing the Future: Building a Legacy of Positivity

The journey you've embarked upon is a testament to your resilience and determination. As we look towards the future, it's essential to cultivate a legacy of positivity that will inspire and uplift those who follow in your footsteps. Embracing the future means acknowledging the challenges that lie ahead while firmly believing in the power of hope and optimism. It's about laying the groundwork for a brighter tomorrow, not just for yourself but for the communities and individuals touched by your endeavors. Every step you take today paves the way for a more vibrant and inclusive future.

Building a legacy of positivity begins with nurturing meaningful connections and fostering an environment of empathy and support. By championing inclusivity and kindness, you create ripples of positive change that extend far beyond your immediate sphere of influence. Your commitment to uplifting others serves as a beacon of hope in a world that often grapples with uncertainty and adversity. Embrace the opportunity to be a catalyst for positivity, knowing that each act of kindness contributes to the greater tapestry of goodness that weaves through humanity.

In crafting a legacy of positivity, it's crucial to instill a mindset of abundance and gratitude. Celebrate your achievements, both big and small, and acknowledge the collective efforts that have brought you to this point. Recognize the value of collaboration and mutual upliftment as indispensable tools in shaping a legacy that transcends individual success. By fostering an attitude of appreciation and thankfulness, you set the stage for a culture of positivity that resonates throughout every endeavor you pursue. Reflect on the multitude of blessings in your life, and let that awareness fuel your passion for creating lasting, positive change.

Embracing the future also involves envisioning the impact of your actions and decisions for generations to come. Consider the footprint you wish to leave on the world and strive to shape it with purposeful positivity. To build a legacy that endures, infuse your endeavors with a spirit of generosity and altruism. Whether through mentorship, philanthropy, or leading by example, embrace the responsibility to uplift others and stimulate progress in ways that ripple across time and space. Your legacy of positivity becomes a timeless echo of the good you sow, perpetuating joy, resilience, and inspiration for all who encounter its path.

As you continue crafting your success story, remember that your legacy is not measured solely by material gains or accomplishments. It is profoundly shaped by the impact you leave on hearts and minds, the enduring imprints of positivity and benevolence that transcend any fleeting accolades. Take pride in your role as a purveyor of positivity, and let this consciousness guide your actions as you weave a legacy that echoes through the ages.

Outro

"If this connected with you, keep reading — I have a few things for you before you go."

Here Is Your Call to Action – Launch Your Next Chapter!

You don't have to make the same mistakes I did.

If this book hit close to home — it's because I've been exactly where you are.

I help founders, freelancers, and first-time entrepreneurs go from zero to 1, and from the first dollar to the first million dollars — using the same principles I wish I knew from day one.

I've worked alongside some of the greatest business developers in the world, and now I take the same frameworks that make billionaires and put them in the hands of first-time entrepreneurs.

Starting the first chapter or launching the next chapter is only an action step away from reality.

Visit MarketChoir.ai slash action, to get free tools, business frameworks, and access to coaching.

Want more books like this — or on other topics?

Visit CounselWolf.com and explore the full catalog.

Coaching. Consulting. Software. Tools that work — built by someone who's been through it.

About the Author

Ralph Skrzypczak is the founder of ATLB Productions, a strategy and systems company built to help small business owners get unstuck and launch with clarity. He's also the creator of Market Choir, a powerful automation platform designed to help first-time entrepreneurs organize, grow, and monetize their business from day one.

Ralph has built and rebuilt everything from restaurants and retail brands to online publishing systems and automation pipelines. Today, he helps others go from zero to $1 million, through a combination of coaching, consulting, DIY, and done-for-you digital systems.

He's worked with some of the world's top business developers, learning firsthand how billion-dollar strategies are formed — and now he brings those same tools to first-time founders, underdogs, and purpose-driven creators.

Through Counsel Wolf Books, Market Choir, and ATLB Productions, Ralph helps people launch smarter, automate faster, and grow with confidence.

Learn more and get free resources at MarketChoir.ai

Lastly, Whatever You Do, Don't Do, What I Did!

Thank you for reading.

The End.

...for now.